12/08

FOSSIL RIDGE PUBLIC LIBRARY DISTRICT

P9-CRI-808

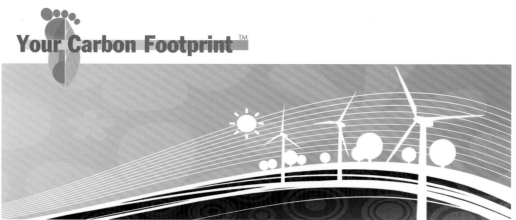

Your Carbon Footprint™

Reducing Your Carbon Footprint
at Home

Sarah B. David

rosen publishing's
rosen central®

New York

Fossil Ridge Public Library District
Braidwood, IL 60408

To Dad

Published in 2009 by The Rosen Publishing Group, Inc.
29 East 21st Street, New York, NY 10010

Copyright © 2009 by The Rosen Publishing Group, Inc.

First Edition

All rights reserved. No part of this book may be reproduced in any form without permission in writing from the publisher, except by a reviewer.

Library of Congress Cataloging-in-Publication Data

David, Sarah B.
Reducing your carbon footprint at home / Sarah B. David.—1st ed.
    p. cm.—(Your carbon footprint)
Includes bibliographical references and index.
ISBN-13: 978-1-4042-1772-0 (lib. bdg.)
1. Energy conservation. 2. Water conservation. 3. Recycling (Waste, etc.).
4. Greenhouse effect, Atmospheric. 5. Sustainable living. I. Title.
TJ163.3.G36 2008
640—dc22
                                                                    2008002118

Manufactured in the United States of America

On the cover: Left: A family separates its trash for recycling. Right: Bottles of different materials to be separated for recycling. Bottom: An energy-efficient home that utilizes solar panels.

Contents

Introduction

Something strange is happening to our planet. Our atmosphere—the air surrounding Earth—is warming up. This transformation is commonly known as global warming.

Scientists agree that higher temperatures are causing big changes on Earth. Earth's glaciers—large sheets of very slow-moving ice—are melting. Sea ice in the Arctic Ocean is gradually shrinking. Storms are getting bigger, droughts longer, and massive heat waves more common.

Global warming is already affecting the world's wildlife. As arctic ice melts, animals like polar bears are threatened with extinction. As the ocean heats up, beautiful coral reefs are dying off. On land, animals and plants adapted to temperate climates are being forced to migrate. According to *Nature* magazine, at least 279 species of plants and animals whose natural habitats have become too hot have started moving to cooler climates closer to Earth's poles. Still other species have nowhere to go. *Nature* also reports that at least seventy species of frogs, mostly from cool climates, have gone extinct due to climate change.

These changes are just the tip of the melting iceberg, however. Global warming may have even more dramatic conse-quences in the future. As our planet's ice melts, our ocean levels will rise. Higher seas could flood coastal cities. Warmer

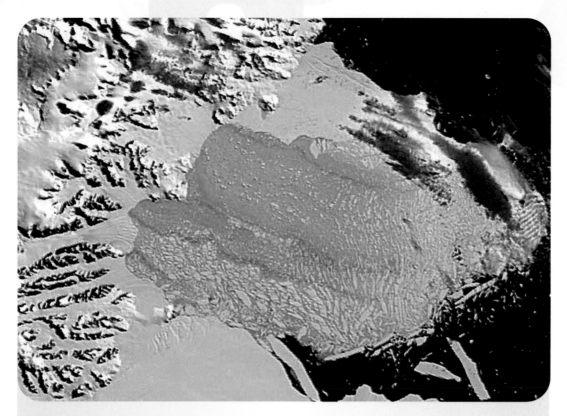

As our planet's atmosphere warms, our glaciers and ice caps melt. In early 2002, the massive Larsen B ice shelf broke off from Antarctica, releasing 720 billion tons of ice into the ocean.

temperatures will change our seasons and could affect human agriculture. Further animal and plant extinctions are likely. And catastrophic hurricanes, tornadoes, and disease epidemics will become more common.

How can we stop global warming and reduce our so-called "carbon footprint"? What does "carbon footprint" mean, and how does carbon relate to global warming and climate change? In order to answer these questions, we first need to know how the warming process, or the greenhouse effect, works.

Carbon and Our Warming Atmosphere

The greenhouse effect is what makes life on Earth possible. When sunlight falls on Earth's surface, most of it is reflected back into space. But certain gases in our atmosphere absorb some sunlight. These "greenhouse gases" trap light and heat inside our atmosphere. The major greenhouse gases include water vapor, carbon dioxide, methane, and nitrous oxide.

Without the greenhouse effect, Earth would be the same freezing temperature as outer space. No plants could grow, and no animals could survive. However, over the last century, human activities have radically increased the amount of greenhouse gases in our atmosphere. More greenhouse gases absorb more of the sun's light and heat, warming our climate even further. Now, Earth is starting to overheat.

Human Impact on the Atmosphere

Over the course of our planet's history, Earth's atmosphere has warmed up and cooled down many times. Changes in the planet's orbit, volcanic eruptions, and collisions with asteroids have all temporarily affected the climate. But the vast majority

During the Industrial Revolution, factories sprung up across Europe and America. This anonymous nineteenth-century lithograph shows factories in Prussia producing coke, a highly processed form of coal.

of scientists agree that today's global warming is caused by human activity.

During the Industrial Revolution, which began around 1760, Europeans and Americans began burning coal for a variety of purposes. Coal provided heat and light to ordinary people, powered steam engines and trains, and fueled factories that created iron and mass-produced goods. Coal helped transform western Europe and the United States into modern industrialized societies. But burning coal releases large amounts of carbon dioxide, a greenhouse gas, into the atmosphere. Our use of coal (and, later, other fossil fuels like oil and natural gas) began the process of global warming.

As living conditions in the West improved, the human population grew larger. More people require more food, so agriculture expanded. But many forms of agriculture produce another greenhouse gas: methane. As new industries grew and developed, new greenhouse gases were added to the atmosphere, such as nitrous oxide, which is created by many industrial activities.

The Carbon Cycle

Carbon is one of the universe's most important elements. It is a vital part of life on Earth. When the planet is healthy, the amount of carbon in our world is kept in balance by the carbon cycle. Carbon atoms circulate between the atmosphere, geosphere (rock and Earth's interior), biosphere (plant and animal life), and the hydrosphere (water such as oceans, lakes, and groundwater). For example, plants take carbon dioxide from the air and release oxygen. When those plants die and decay, some of the carbon they contain is released back into the atmosphere, while the rest becomes a part of the ground.

Large reservoirs of carbon are contained within our planet as fossil fuels. Coal, oil, and natural gas are three major fossil fuels. They were formed during the carboniferous period, 354 to 290 million years ago. At that time, Earth was covered with swamps containing huge trees and ferns, while the sea was full of algae. When these plants and algae died,

Global carbon cycle

Carbon dioxide (CO_2) is responsible for more than 60% of the greenhouse effect; humans are upsetting carbon cycle, a precisely balanced system by which carbon is exchanged between air, ocean and land:

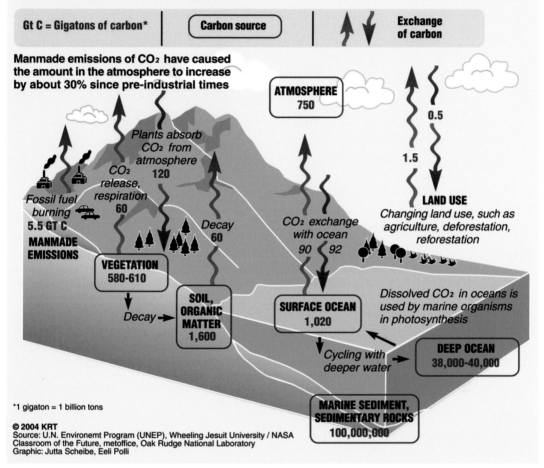

Gt C = Gigatons of carbon* | Carbon source | Exchange of carbon

Manmade emissions of CO_2 have caused the amount in the atmosphere to increase by about 30% since pre-industrial times

ATMOSPHERE
750

0.5

1.5

Plants absorb
CO_2 from
atmosphere
120

CO_2
release,
respiration
60

Fossil fuel
burning
5.5 GT C

MANMADE
EMISSIONS

LAND USE
Changing land use, such as
agriculture, deforestation,
reforestation

Decay
60

CO_2 exchange
with ocean
90 92

VEGETATION
580-610

Decay

SOIL,
ORGANIC
MATTER
1,600

SURFACE OCEAN
1,020

Dissolved CO_2 in oceans is
used by marine organisms
in photosynthesis

Cycling with
deeper water

DEEP OCEAN
38,000-40,000

*1 gigaton = 1 billion tons

MARINE SEDIMENT,
SEDIMENTARY ROCKS
100,000,000

© 2004 KRT
Source: U.N. Environemt Program (UNEP), Wheeling Jesuit University / NASA
Classroom of the Future, metoffice, Oak Rudge National Laboratory
Graphic: Jutta Scheibe, Eeli Polli

The carbon cycle normally keeps Earth's carbon in balance by shifting it from land to sea to air and back again. When we burn fossil fuels, we add more carbon dioxide to the air than the carbon cycle can process.

Carbon Calculators

There are a number of Web sites that can help you calculate your carbon footprint. These "carbon calculators" take into account the number of people who live in your home, your driving habits, how much electricity and gas you use at home, and whether or not you recycle. The calculator will then tell you how many pounds of greenhouse gases (expressed as carbon dioxide equivalents) you emit every year. The calculator may also show you how making certain lifestyle changes could subtract pounds of carbon from your footprint.

they sank to the bottom of Earth's swamps and oceans. Over thousands of years, the plant remains were gradually covered by rock and soil. Under geological pressure, they became fossil fuels. When we burn fossil fuels, we release the carbon they store into our atmosphere. The burning of carbon creates the greenhouse gas carbon dioxide.

Carbon Out of Balance

Today, humans release more carbon dioxide and methane (a gas that includes carbon) than ever into the atmosphere. It's too much for the carbon cycle to absorb. According to the Intergovernmental Panel on Climate Change, in the years since the Industrial Revolution, the amount of carbon dioxide in our atmosphere has increased 31 percent.

Trees and plants absorb carbon in the atmosphere and release oxygen. But as human populations grow, more and more trees are cut down to clear room for agriculture and cities, to provide fuel, and to become raw materials for buildings, homes, and products. With more carbon released into our atmosphere and less forests to absorb it, it's no wonder that Earth is heating up.

Carbon Footprint

You may not know it, but you release carbon into the atmosphere every day. You might ride in a car that runs on gasoline and burns oil, switch on a light powered by coal-generated electricity, or turn on a heater that burns natural gas.

Your carbon footprint is the amount of carbon that your activities emit (or contribute to the atmosphere). Luckily, you can reduce your carbon footprint by paying attention to what you buy, how you travel, and what you throw away. It's part of a worldwide movement some people call "going green." A "green" lifestyle can help you become healthier, wealthier, and happier.

2 | Saving Energy

Whenever you turn on a light, when you put food in the refrigerator, or when you watch television, listen to music, or check your e-mail, you are using electricity. Although you may not think about it often, all that electricity comes from somewhere, and generating it can have a profound impact upon the environment and Earth's atmosphere.

The Cost of Electricity

According to the Environmental Protection Agency (EPA), electricity generation was responsible for 40 percent of the United States' 2004 greenhouse gas emissions (the amount of greenhouse gases released into the atmosphere). Some of that electricity was used to power factories, streetlights, and other large-scale power needs. But 15 percent of the United States' total emissions comes from the electricity we use in our own homes.

The amount of carbon you release when you use electricity depends on how your electricity was generated. The way that electricity is generated varies from state to state and region to region. In North America, most energy is generated in power plants. Electricity that comes from solar, wind, and nuclear power plants releases comparatively little carbon dioxide. However, most power plants in the United States create energy by burning coal, oil, and natural gas. When these fossil fuels are burned, they release carbon dioxide. According to the Energy Information Administration, in 2006, 49 percent of the United States' electricity was created by burning coal.

Luckily, it is possible to reduce your carbon footprint—and your family's energy bills—by cutting back on the electricity you use at home.

You can save electricity by changing the way you use common household devices, such as refrigerators.

Starting Simple

It's easy to waste energy. Perhaps you leave the television on when no one's watching it or forget to turn off the lights when you leave a room. If you start thinking about how much energy you consume, you'll start finding lots of little ways to save it. For instance, if you have big windows that let in lots of natural light, don't turn on your lights until you need them. At night, make sure that lights are turned off when they are not being used. Switch off the lights whenever you leave an empty room.

You can also save energy by switching to energy-efficient compact fluorescent lightbulbs, or CFLs. CFLs use roughly a fifth of the energy

Compact fluorescent lightbulbs, or CFLs, use less electricity—and hence release less carbon into the atmosphere—than normal incandescent lightbulbs.

of normal lightbulbs, and they last much longer. Look for products labeled with the U.S. government's Energy Star label, which marks energy-efficient products.

Some items, like MP3 power adapters and cell phone chargers, are "energy vampires": they sap electricity as long as they are plugged into your wall, even if they're not actively charging anything. Unplug your chargers from the wall when they are not in use. The same rule applies to computers, televisions, and other large electronics. These items use energy when they are on stand-by mode. Even if they've been turned off, they continue to take energy from your wall. To save energy and money, plug your electronics into a power strip with an on/off button. At the end of the night, turn off your electronics and then turn off the power strip.

Heating Up and Cooling Down

Some houses are heated with gas-burning radiators, which release carbon dioxide into the atmosphere. Other homes use electricity, which also creates carbon emissions. Air conditioners require lots of electricity to run, and some also release chemicals that help destroy the ozone layer, which protects us from harmful ultraviolet radiation.

In cold weather, you can save energy by putting on a sweater rather than turning up the thermostat a few degrees. In summer, you can keep your house comfortable instead of cold.

Changing your heating and cooling habits can shrink your carbon footprint. Many experts on personal emissions recommend moving your thermostat down two degrees in the winter and up two degrees in the summer. Don't waste the heat or cool you create. During the winter, keep the doors between your rooms shut, so that heat doesn't escape from the toasty place in which you are sitting throughout the rest of the house. During the summer, keep the doors between your rooms shut to avoid wasting energy by cooling down unused rooms. When you leave the house, always lower your thermostat in winter and raise it in summer.

Saving Energy in the Kitchen

For further energy savings, pay more attention to how you use your kitchen. When your refrigerator door is left even a tiny bit open, your refrigerator must work overtime to maintain its cool temperature. When you shut your refrigerator door, make sure that it is fully closed. Your

Going Green

People across the world are going green. They're taking action to shrink their own carbon footprints now, before it's too late. John and Cori Fraley of Bothell, Washington, reduced their carbon footprint as part of a *Seattle Times* 2007 challenge to its readers. They cut down their weekly driving time, switched from disposable to cloth diapers, started composting their organic trash, and turned down their thermostat.

In 1998, climatologist Jonathan Foley realized that his own actions were changing the climate. According to *Audubon* magazine, he and his wife, Andrea, decided to reduce their emissions by 50 percent over two years. They replaced many of their old appliances with new, energy-efficient models and switched to solar and wind power.

Author Colin Beavan attempted to make no impact on the environment for one whole year. During his experiment, his family gradually gave up electricity, mechanical transportation, plastic, and more. Beavan wrote on his blog, "No Impact Man": "'The goal' is really just the place where you are really conscious of what you use. You don't take things for granted. You understand that your actions have consequences for other people and the planet." Even communities, towns, and cities are getting in on the act. As of late 2007, hundreds of American mayors had signed the Mayors Climate Protection Agreement, pledging to reduce their own cities' emissions.

parents can also save energy by occasionally vacuuming off the coils on the back of the refrigerator. If you have a gas-burning stove, don't waste gas. When you heat up small portions of food, the microwave actually uses less energy than the oven.

Saving Energy in the Laundry Room

Only run your laundry machine when you have a full load of laundry to wash. Wash as many clothes as possible in cold water: you will save the energy it would otherwise take to heat up your wash water.

The biggest energy-waster in American laundry rooms is the dryer. Air-drying laundry saves lots of electricity. Air-dried clothes also smell nicer, and their colors do not fade as quickly as machine-dried clothes. If it's raining outside, or if you don't have an open-air clothes line, you can dry your clothes inside on a drying rack. If you do use your clothes dryer, remember to clean its filter regularly so that your machine runs as efficiently as possible.

Bigger Changes

If your family is interested in making bigger changes to your home, you can start radically shrinking your family's carbon footprint. And since reducing your carbon footprint means using less energy—which is very expensive—your family will save lots of money that can be better spent elsewhere.

Energy-Efficient Appliances

You can save lots of energy with energy-efficient appliances. The next time your family needs to replace an appliance, choose one that is marked with the Energy Star label. These products meet the EPA's strict rules for energy efficiency. They will save your family both energy and money over time.

Weatherization

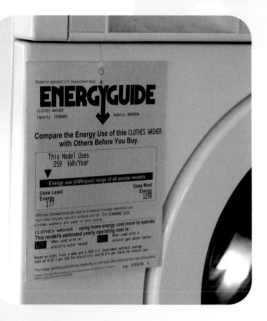

Energy-efficient appliances may be more expensive to buy, but over time they will help your family save money on utilities.

You use lots of energy to heat your home each winter and keep it cool in the summer. Your family can save energy—and money—by weatherizing your home. This means detecting all the places in your home that let in air from the outside and sealing them off. It also means making sure that your home is well insulated. Insulation is material that keeps the climate inside separate from the climate outside, preventing heat from escaping your house in winter and minimizing the heat absorbed by the house from the outside in summer.

Your family can also get a professional "energy audit" to find out how to make your home more energy-efficient. Learn more by contacting your state or local government energy office.

Energy-Efficient Windows

When your family decides to get new windows, save energy by choosing double-paned windows. Single-paned windows are not very efficient at blocking cold air in the winter or keeping out hot air in the summer. Double-paned windows, which consist of two windows separated by a small gas- or air-filled space, are a type of insulation. Do research

Well-insulated homes require less energy to heat and cool. Here, a worker fills the attic of a new house with fiberglass insulation.

before selecting your new double-paned windows: some windows are better suited to specific climates.

Renewable Energy

Carbon emissions are not the only problem with fossil fuels. Fossil fuels are also a limited, or nonrenewable, resource. Because it takes millions of years for fossil fuels to form, they cannot be replaced quickly. One day, humans may completely use up all of Earth's existing fossil fuels.

Solar panels capture the sun's energy and transform it into electricity with photovoltaic cells. Clean, renewable solar power helps reduce the carbon footprint of thousands of Americans.

One of the great challenges of the twenty-first century will be developing renewable energies that will never run out and whose production and use will not harm the environment.

Perhaps the best way to reduce your carbon footprint is to start using cleaner, renewable energy. Solar power, hydropower, wind power, and other renewable energies release far less carbon dioxide into the atmosphere than power generated by burning coal. These forms of energy may have their own environmental problems. For instance, hydropower plants can endanger fish and wildlife. But the energy produced by renewable sources helps to reduce carbon emissions, which are currently the gravest threat to our planet and life upon it.

Do some research and find out what the green power options are available in your area. Your family should ask questions before switching to any new power source. Make sure that you know that the green energy you are buying is really green and that it fits your family budget.

3 | Conserving Water

Saving electricity isn't the only way to reduce your carbon dioxide emissions. Saving water is another important part of shrinking your carbon footprint. To understand why, let's take a closer look at how tap water reaches our houses.

Saving Water, Saving the World

Water uses up energy. In some places with access to clean, natural sources of freshwater, it does not take much energy to deliver water to peoples' homes. But in other locations, water goes through an extensive, energy-consuming purification process before reaching sinks and showers.

Water must be treated to make it safe to drink. Then it must be delivered to reservoirs and, eventually, to our homes. In turn, wastewater from our homes and businesses must be treated before it can be safely returned to nature. According to the California Energy Commission, more than 19 percent of California's total electricity consumption is devoted to water management. When you use water, you're also using the electricity necessary to treat and deliver your water. That electricity contributes to your carbon footprint.

Most groundwater must go through a complex purification process before it reaches your faucets. Every part of the process takes energy.

You also use energy when you use hot water. It takes energy to heat up cold water for showers, dishwashers, and laundry machines. When you use hot water, you are releasing carbon into our atmosphere.

Running Out of Water

Only 1 percent of Earth's freshwater is found in lakes, groundwater, and rivers where humans can use it. The freshwater that is not found in groundwater like lakes and streams is frozen in glaciers and polar ice caps, or underground. The amount of pure freshwater that humans can drink and use for agriculture is limited. Steadily expanding cities and suburbs deplete groundwater supplies and drain lake and river habitats of freshwater animals. As ever-growing human populations require more and more food, the water required to grow crops adequate to feed billions of people is increasingly in danger, especially in naturally dry environments. Experts warn that the world may soon face a critical water shortage. To meet the challenges of the future, we must get serious about saving water.

Saving Water in the Bathroom

One of the best places to start saving water is in your bathroom. According to the Discovery Channel's *Planet Green*, a dripping faucet can waste twenty gallons of water a day. Leaky toilets may waste up to ninety thousand gallons of water in just one month. This wasted clean water must be treated and goes through the system just like dirty water does.

Another big water-waster is your shower. It feels great to shower, and lots of people stay in the shower longer than it takes for them to clean off. You might want to use a shower-safe timer to make sure that you don't

You can help save water by turning off the faucet when you are brushing your teeth or soaping up dishes.

stay in the shower too long. Consider making your shower a bit cooler to save hot water. Save water by installing a low-flow showerhead. Low-flow showerheads that have earned the Energy Star label restrict the flow of your shower to two-and-a-half gallons of water per minute or less.

Saving Water in the Kitchen

When hand-washing your dishes, scrape off the dishes before putting them in the sink so that it takes less time and water to wash them. Instead of filling up your entire sink with hot water when you wash dishes, get a big bowl and fill that with water. Save hot water by rinsing your dishes off in cold water.

If you use a dishwasher, then you should only run it with a full load. According to *Consumer Reports'* Greener Choices Web site, your dishwasher will clean your dishes just as well without prerinsing. By not prerinsing, you could save up to 6,500 gallons of water per year.

When your family is looking for your next washing machine, toilet, or dishwasher, consider buying a water-saving model. Look for the Energy Star label to choose an efficient, more Earth-friendly machine.

Saving Water in the Garden

If you've got a lawn or garden, think of ways to save water. For instance, most lawns don't need to be watered every day. Watering only once every three days encourages grass roots to grow deeper into the ground. That means your lawn can use the water it gets more efficiently. When you do water, do it at night or in the early morning. This will prevent evaporation and allow more water to reach the roots of your grass.

Many people who live in very dry climates use thirsty plants from far-away, colder places in their gardens. These plants need lots of water to survive. One green gardening tip is to use plants native to your area, which are already adapted to the local environment and climate. Native plants often need less water and can survive with less artificial watering, instead relying on rainfall for hydration.

Planting a tree is a long-term way to reduce your carbon footprint. When you add trees to your lawn and garden, you remove carbon dioxide from the atmosphere. You also create shade and shelter for other plants in your garden. Well-placed trees near doors and windows can help lower your house's electricity bill by cooling your house in the summer.

Going Further in the Garden: Gray Water and Rainwater

If you want to revolutionize your water use, consider gray water and rainwater systems. These are water-saving solutions that will help reduce your dependence on the water system. If you live in a house with rain gutters, you can place barrels under their spouts to collect rainwater. This rainwater can later be used to water the plants in your garden.

In addition, some green people harvest and use gray water. Gray water is water that has been used for brushing teeth, bathing, and washing dishes and clothes, but it is still clean enough to use for other purposes. Gray water should not be confused with black water, which is water from the toilet that cannot be reused until it has been treated extensively. Reusing gray water may be as simple as keeping a container in the shower to collect excess water, which can later be used for shaving. Or, it could mean watering your garden with dirty water from a fish tank.

Trees absorb carbon dioxide from the atmosphere and release oxygen in its place.

There are many gray water dos and don'ts. If you're interested in gray water, learn about how to reuse it safely, legally, and efficiently. Do your research about whether or not gray water is right for you.

Putting Down the Bottle

One way to reduce your carbon footprint is to stop buying bottled water. The Union of Concerned Scientists reports that bottled water is not necessarily healthier or more pure than tap water. In fact, tap water is monitored more strictly than bottled water. Plus, nearly 90 percent of water bottles are not recycled. Instead, they are thrown into landfills, where they won't decompose for hundreds of years. Start bringing tap water with you in a reusable plastic or metal bottle. You'll save money, save water, and reduce the amount of waste dumped upon our fragile planet.

4 | Reducing Consumption and Reusing Products

I t's easy to understand how we emit carbon when we switch on a lightbulb or turn on a water tap. But there are also hidden carbon costs associated with everything that we buy, from new printer paper to a cup of coffee. In modern times, we ordinarily buy our clothes, our tools, our food, and the other items that make our lives possible, rather than produce them ourselves. It takes energy to make these products, to transport them to stores, and to dispose of them when they are no longer needed. Therefore, consuming fewer products reduces your carbon footprint.

The Hidden Costs of Food

In today's globalized world, a family in Minnesota can buy pasta from Italy, soy sauce from China, and avocados from Israel all in the same store. But we seldom think about how far that food had to travel to reach us. According to the Worldwatch Institute, the average American meal travels two thousand miles from farm to table. The energy spent on this transportation and shipping releases carbon dioxide into our atmosphere.

Bales of cardboard are stacked up at a recycling center. According to the EPA, recycling 500 tons of paper removes as much carbon dioxide from our atmosphere as does taking 259 cars off the road for a year.

Many foods come wrapped in elaborate packaging. It takes energy and resources to create this packaging. Let's imagine a cardboard cereal box. Its life cycle begins when trees are chopped down and taken to a paper factory. There, the trees are transformed into paper pulp, then shaped into boxes. At every stage of the production process, the coal-powered cereal box factory creates greenhouse gas emissions. Once finished, the cereal box is transported thousands of miles to a store. It is sold, used, and thrown away within a few days. The box is then picked up by a garbage truck, which produces even more carbon emissions. If the box is not recycled, it will be burned, releasing carbon dioxide, or sent to a landfill, where it will help produce the greenhouse gas methane as it decomposes. When we reduce the amount of waste we create, we shrink our carbon footprints.

Making Smart Choices

You can reduce your carbon footprint by becoming a smart consumer. Avoid disposable products whenever possible. For instance, cloth kitchen towels can clean up most nasty messes in the kitchen. They can

Meat

Meat production takes a much heavier environmental toll than the growing of fruits and vegetables. Meat production uses lots of fossil fuels. According to the Sierra Club, a gallon of oil is needed to produce every pound of beef. In fact, according to the Worldwatch Institute, 16 percent of the greenhouse gases generated by humans across the globe have their roots in the livestock industry. The president of the environmental Web site Grist.org, Chip Giller, adds that if every American stopped eating meat just once a week, the carbon emissions savings to the country would equal the removal of 8 million cars from the road.

be washed and used again afterward. You can cut back on waste by not using disposable plastic and paper shopping bags. When you go to the grocery story, bring a reusable canvas or nylon shopping bag from home.

Before you buy a product, look at the packaging it comes in. If you have a choice between two similar products, choose the product that can be reused or the product that comes in less wasteful packaging. For example, if you're buying a new pen, buy one that can be refilled with new ink cartridges. Avoid buying disposable pens and pens that come in cardboard and plastic packages. One good way to reduce the amount of packaging you consume is to buy in bulk. Many products, including cereal, snacks, and coffee, can be bought with no packaging at all, using containers that you bring from home.

You can also help save the planet by choosing green products. From recycled Tupperware to organic insect repellents, there are lots of Earth-friendly products offered by companies that want to make a difference.

Reducing and Reusing in the Home Office

Many people use home offices for work and school. Unfortunately, many home offices create lots of waste. One good example is paper used for printing out homework, e-mails, reports, documents, and other items. Paper production is a major burden on our planet. According to the Sierra Club, the pulp and paper industry is the second-biggest industrial consumer of energy in the United States.

Reducing the amount of paper you use can help cut your carbon footprint down to size. Read the newspaper online. Reduce the number of items that you print out. If you must print, use double-sided printing, and recycle the paper afterward. Reuse your scrap paper. Cancel your catalog subscriptions to save even more paper.

Reducing and Reusing in the Kitchen

There are even more ways to reduce your carbon footprint in the kitchen. Try to avoid snack foods that come wrapped in individual packages. Use reusable coffee cups and water bottles. According to San José's *Metroactive* magazine, buying coffee in a disposable cup every day will create at least twenty pounds of paper waste over the course of a year.

As already mentioned, buying food that is grown or produced far away adds to your carbon footprint, since the food must be transported to your table. Whenever possible, buy locally grown and produced food.

Thousands of farmer's markets operate across the United States, allowing farmers to sell fresh, healthy products directly to customers.

One great place to find locally grown food is at your local farmer's market. By buying food from local farmers, you'll reduce your carbon footprint and help support your local farmers. Locally grown food is often also healthier, fresher, and tastier.

5 | Recycling and Beyond

Reducing and reusing your waste can drastically cut down on the amount of items you throw in the trash. In addition, there's a third way to reduce your waste and your carbon footprint: recycling.

A number of materials, like glass, aluminum, paper, and many kinds of plastic, can be recycled. Recycling stops us from throwing away materials that could be made into something new. When you send glass to be recycled, for example, it is melted down and used to create new glass.

Recycling reduces the amount of trash that we send to landfills and incinerators. Recycling also reduces the amount of raw material required to create new products. It even takes less energy to manufacture products out of recycled materials. Here are a few of the items that can take on new life through recycling.

Aluminum

Aluminum is one of the easiest and most profitable materials to recycle. Recycling aluminum is efficient, cost-effective, and widespread. According to the *Economist*, it takes 95 percent less energy to make an aluminum can out of recycled materials than out of new materials. And the Aluminum Association tells us that when you recycle one aluminum can, you are saving enough energy to run a television for three hours.

Paper

Paper recycling is less efficient than aluminum recycling, but it is just as important. When you recycle paper, you are reducing the paper industry's need to cut down more trees. According to *National Geographic*'s *The Green Guide*, nearly half of the trees cut down in North America are used to make paper. Recycling paper helps reduce the demand for virgin wood. This is particu-

It's good recycling etiquette to remove labels, lids, and caps from your products. Rinse out your jars and cans before dropping them into the recycling bin.

larly important from an emissions point of view, since trees transform carbon dioxide into oxygen. In addition, logging and timber transportation require the burning of large amounts of fossil fuels, adding more carbon to the atmosphere that these cut trees can no longer absorb.

Glass

Some glass bottles are returnable. When possible, it's better to return bottles than to recycle them. Returned glass bottles are rinsed and reused for their original purpose, a less energy-intensive process than recycling. However, glass can be recycled many, many times. Glass bottles are melted down and then used to create new glass bottles. Recycled glass can also be used to create ceramics, bricks, and more.

Plastic

Plastic is one of the most important and most challenging materials to recycle. When you throw plastic bottles into the trash, they are taken to landfills. There, it will take seven hundred years before they even begin the extremely long process of decomposition. On the other hand, recycled plastic can be used to make lots of different types of products, from bottles to sleeping-bag filling to T-shirts.

There are seven different types of plastic. Not all of them are commonly recycled. Take a look at the plastic item you want to recycle to find out what type of plastic it is. Somewhere on the product, you should find a small triangle with a number in the center. This identifies the type of plastic you're looking at. The most commonly recycled plastics are plastics #1 and #2. Make sure you know what types of plastic your local recycling program accepts. If you try to recycle types of plastic your local recycler cannot handle, they will just be tossed in the trash anyway.

Other Items

Other materials that can be recycled include heavy electronics, ink cartridges, batteries, paint, motor oil, textiles, and even timber. Do some

Recycling makes use of the plastic that already exists and prevents it from becoming just trash.

research and find out where and how to recycle these materials in your community.

How Do I Recycle?

The first step is to find out what recycling programs are available in your area and how they work. Many neighborhoods offer curbside recycling pickup. This means that you can set out recycling in a special

Many ink and toner cartridges can be refilled and reused by the manufacturer. When you buy new ink cartridges, check the packaging for recycling instructions.

bin next to your trash can. In some places, you can throw trash and recycling into one container—professionals will sort them out later on. In some areas with no curbside pickup, you may need to bring your recycling to a recycling center. If there are no recycling programs near you, you might be able to work with friends, with your school, or with a local business to start a recycling program.

Find out how your local recycling program works. Don't recycle items your local program can't handle. Use good recycling etiquette by removing labels and lids from your bottles and jars and rinsing them out before you recycle them.

Buying Recycled Products

Another important aspect of recycling is buying products made from recycled materials. When you go shopping for printer paper, notebooks, bottles, and even clothes, check the labels of products. Look for items that were made from recycled materials (often referred to as "Recycled-Content Products" or "Postconsumer Content").

Composting

Another way of reusing waste from your kitchen and your yard is composting. Compost is a mixture of decaying organic matter (plant and animal residues). Mature compost is produced when helpful bacteria break down your organic trash to make a type of rich fertilizer. Mature compost can keep your plants healthy and your garden green. It also helps eliminate some of the greenhouse gases that your waste would otherwise release into the atmosphere while rotting.

Composting methods range from very simple "passive composting"—which could be as basic as just making a pile of lawn trimmings and leaving it to rot—to complex compost piles that need lots of attention. The list of materials that can and cannot be composted is surprising. For instance, you can compost clean paper, cardboard rolls, sawdust, tea bags, wood chips, and lint from your dryer. However, selected materials might be dangerous to compost, such as black walnut bark and leaves, dairy products, fat, oil, meat, and fish bones. Before you and your family start composting, learn how to do so safely and effectively.

Mulching

One way of reusing garden trimmings is mulching. Mulch is a thin layer of organic matter spread out over the face of the ground. Over time, mulch decays and helps to enrich the soil while protecting plants. Common mulches are wood chips, grass, and sawdust. Sprinkling grass clippings over the face of your lawn is one easy way to mulch.

According to the EPA, 24 percent of the United States' solid waste stream is made up of yard trimmings and food leftovers. Mulching and composting help keep organic waste out of landfills.

Be the Change You Want to See

You can urge your school to do its part by reducing the amount of paper it uses, conserving energy, and increasing its energy efficiency. Make sure your school recycles paper, bottles, and cans. Encourage your school to buy green paper products made from recycled material. Write a letter or an e-mail to your state representatives. Ask them to support strong measures to develop alternative renewable energy and to reduce emissions both state- and nationwide.

Above all, stay informed, involved, and active. Always ask yourself what effect your actions are having on the environment. The problem of global warming is enormous, but every solution has to start somewhere. Your actions could inspire other people to change their own lives.

Start small. By changing your life one habit, one product at a time, you can make a difference. If everyone pitches in to reduce his or her own carbon footprint, we can help make the world a better, cleaner, healthier, and greener place. By reducing, reusing, and recycling, we can even save lives—our own, our planet's, those of all living things, and those of future generations on Earth.

Glossary

agriculture The practice of growing fruits and vegetables or raising animals for meat, milk, eggs, and other food items. Agriculture can also refer to cultivating land or raising animals in order to make building materials, clothing, or other products.

atmosphere The layer of gases surrounding a planet or other large heavenly body.

carbon The sixth-most-common element in the universe. Solid carbon can take the form of charcoal, diamonds, and graphite, among other materials.

carbon dioxide A gas made from one carbon atom and two oxygen atoms. Carbon dioxide is exhaled by animals and absorbed by plants. Carbon dioxide is an important greenhouse gas. When humans burn fossil fuels in order to create electricity or to fuel machinery, they release carbon dioxide into the atmosphere.

carbon footprint The estimated total amount of carbon dioxide released into the atmosphere by a person, group, or product. Activities that burn fossil fuels, consume energy and/or water, and produce needless waste add to one's carbon footprint. Activities that reduce waste, save energy, and conserve water reduce one's carbon footprint.

climate The weather in a specific place (or the whole planet) measured over a certain period of time.

compact fluorescent lightbulb (CFL) A simple, energy-efficient, longer-lasting replacement for regular lightbulbs.

compost A rich fertilizer made out of decaying organic materials. Composting is an alternative way to dispose of biodegradable trash, such as some kinds of food and yard trimmings. Instead of going to a landfill or an incinerator, composted waste is placed in a large pile, where, over time, it naturally decomposes and becomes fertilizer.

emissions When referring to the climate, emissions are the amount of greenhouse gases released into the atmosphere over a period of time in a certain location or by a certain activity.

energy-efficient Characterized by high activity but low energy usage. Any energy-consuming item that makes a little power go a long way is energy-efficient. Energy-efficient products use a smaller-than-normal amount of electricity and waste very little of the power they consume.

Energy Star A U.S. government program that helps individuals and businesses save energy and money over the long term. Energy Star labels energy-efficient products in order to allow consumers to make more informed choices.

farmer's market A usually outdoor market where consumers can buy local farm products. Farmer's markets are held across North America.

fossil fuels Fuels rich in carbon—the remains of ancient plant and animal life from thousands of years ago. When fossil fuels are burned to provide heat or energy, they release carbon dioxide, a greenhouse gas, into the atmosphere. Common fossil fuels are coal, oil, and natural gas.

gray water Water used for cleaning people or clothes, then reused for other purposes (filling toilet tanks, irrigating plants, etc.). It does not include black water, which is water from the toilet.

greenhouse gas A gas that absorbs energy from the sun and prevents this heat from leaving Earth's atmosphere. Common greenhouse gases include methane, carbon dioxide, and water vapor.

groundwater The pure water stored beneath Earth's surface.

Industrial Revolution The period of time (beginning around the 1760s and lasting through the late nineteenth century) when western Europe and America began shifting from small-scale agricultural economies to economies centered around mass manufacturing.

livestock Domestic animals raised on a farm, such as chickens, cows, pigs, etc.

methane A greenhouse gas. Human activities that emit methane include the raising of livestock, growing rice, coal mining, sewage treatment, and disposing of waste in landfills.

migrate To travel to a new area in order to survive. Species migrate for a number of reasons, including overpopulation, food shortages, inhospitable weather, etc. Some animals migrate seasonally, moving every year in order to breed, feed, etc.

mulch Organic material such as straw, grass clippings, or tree bark scattered on the soil around a plant. Mulch protects soil and plant roots, aids in moisture retention, and is a natural way to dispose of certain organic materials.

nitrous oxide A greenhouse gas produced by nitrogen-based fertilizers, sewage treatment, animal manure management, and other sources.

recycling The transformation of trash into raw materials for new products.

renewable energy Sources of energy that naturally renew themselves and are, in theory, impossible to deplete, such as solar energy, wind energy, and hydropower.

weatherize To seal up leaks and drafts in a building, insulate it, and generally protect an interior from extreme weather conditions and temperatures.

For More Information

Environmental Defence Canada

317 Adelaide Street West, Suite 705

Toronto, ON M5V 1P9

Canada

(416) 323-9521

Web site: http://www.environmentaldefence.ca

This Canadian organization works to raise awareness of environmental issues among people, businesses, and governments. One of its special focuses is the greening of cities.

Natural Resources Defense Council (NRDC)

40 West 20th Street

New York, NY 10011

(212) 727-2700

Web site: http://www.nrdc.org

The environmental organization NRDC works vigorously to help create new laws, raise awareness, and effect change in a number of ways. With a staff of lawyers, scientists, and policy experts, the NRDC works on issues from decreasing the use of toxic chemicals in the United States to urging China to reduce its greenhouse gas emissions.

Pew Center on Global Climate Change

2101 Wilson Boulevard, Suite 550

Arlington, VA 22201

(703) 516-4146

Web site: http://www.pewclimate.org

The Pew Center on Global Climate Change is an organization that promotes the development of new and innovative solutions to the challenges presented by global warming.

U.S. Environmental Protection Agency (EPA)
Ariel Rios Building
1200 Pennsylvania Avenue NW
Washington, DC 20460
(800) 424-4372
Web site: http://www.epa.gov
Founded in 1970, the EPA is a government agency whose mission is to protect the United States' environment and the health of its citizens. Among other activities, it promotes environmental education and makes relevant information available to the public.

Web Sites

Due to the changing nature of Internet links, Rosen Publishing has developed an online list of Web sites related to the subject of this book. This site is updated regularly. Please use this link to access the list:

http://www.rosenlinks.com/ycf/atho

For Further Reading

David, Laurie, and Cambria Gordon. *The Down-to-Earth Guide to Global Warming*. New York, NY: Orchard Books, 2007.

Gore, Al. *Earth in the Balance: Ecology and the Human Spirit*. New York, NY: Rodale Books, 2006.

Gore, Al. *An Inconvenient Truth: The Crisis of Global Warming*. New York, NY: Rodale Books, 2006.

Grist Magazine, Brangien Davis, and Katharine Wroth, eds. *Wake Up and Smell the Planet*. Seattle, WA: Mountaineers Books, 2007.

Langholz, Jeffrey, and Kelly Turner. *You Can Prevent Global Warming (and Save Money!): 51 Easy Ways*. Kansas City, MO: Andrews McMeel Publishing, 2003.

Spence, Christopher. *Global Warming: Personal Solutions for a Healthy Planet*. New York, NY: Palgrave MacMillan, 2005.

Thornhill, Jan. *This Is My Planet: The Kids' Guide to Global Warming*. Toronto, ON: Maple Tree Press, 2007.

Trask, Crissy. *It's Easy Being Green: A Handbook for Earth-Friendly Living*. Layton, UT: Gibbs Smith, 2006.

Bibliography

Brower, Michael, and Warren Leon. *The Consumer's Guide to Effective Environmental Choices: Practical Advice from the Union of Concerned Scientists*. New York, NY: Three Rivers Press, 1999.

Clean Air-Cool Planet. "What Is Global Warming?" Retrieved December 22, 2007 (http://www.cleanair-coolplanet.org/information/index.php).

Consumer Reports Greener Choices. "Everyday Water-Saving Tips." July 2005. Retrieved December 22, 2007 (http://www.greenerchoices.org/products.cfm?product=watersaving&pcat=homegarden).

Friend, Robyn, and Judith Love Cohen. *A Clean Sky: The Global Warming Story*. Marina del Rey, CA: Cascade Pass, 2007.

Gershon, David. *Low Carbon Diet*. Woodstock, NY: Empowerment Institute, 2006.

Horn, Greg. *Living Green: A Practical Guide to Simple Sustainability*. Topanga, CA: Freedom Press, 2006.

Karlstrom, Solvie. "Tapped Out: The True Cost of Bottled Water." *The Green Guide*, July/August 2007. Retrieved December 22, 2007 (http://www.thegreenguide.com/doc/121/bottle).

Kondratyev, Kirill Ya., Vladmir F. Krapivin, and Costas A. Varatsos. *Global Carbon Cycle and Climate Change*. New York, NY: Springer, 2003.

Main, Emily, and P. W. McRandle. "A Calculated Loss: How to Reduce Your Global Warming Emissions." *The Green Guide*, March/April 2007. Retrieved December 2007 (http://www.thegreenguide.com/doc/119/calculator).

The Nature Conservancy. "Climate Change: What You Can Do. Fast Facts About Climate Change." Retrieved December 22, 2007 (http://www.nature.org/initiatives/climatechange/activities/art19631.html).

Rogers, Elizabeth, and Thomas M Kostigen. *The Green Book: The Everyday Guide to Saving the Planet One Simple Step at a Time.* New York, NY: Three Rivers Press, 2007.

Sierra Club. "Global Population and Environment: Population, Consumption and Our Ecological Footprint." November 21, 2006. Retrieved December 22, 2007 (http://www.commondreams.org/headlines06/1121-09.htm).

Sierra Club. "Sustainable Consumption: Energy Consumption and Its Environmental Impact." Retrieved December 22, 2007 (http://www.sierraclub.org/sustainable%5Fconsumption/factsheets/energy_factsheet.asp).

Sierra Club. "Sustainable Consumption: Food Consumption and Its Environmental Impact." Retrieved December 22, 2007 (http://www.sierraclub.org/sustainable%5Fconsumption/factsheets/food_factsheet.asp).

Solomon, Diane. "50 Ways to Reduce Your Carbon Footprint." *Metroactive*, August 15–21, 2007. Retrieved December 22, 2007 (http://www.metroactive.com/metro/08.15.07/50-ways-to-go-green-0733.html).

Taylor, David. "Eco Homes: 20 Ways to Make Your Home Greener." October 13, 2007. Retrieved December 22, 2007 (http://www.telegraph.co.uk/property/main.jhtml?xml=/property/2007/10/13/pgreener113.xml&page=1).

Index

About the Author

Sarah B. David is an author and educator from Oakland, California. She writes about science history and endangered animals for young audiences. Many of her family members and friends work for environmental organizations such as the Sierra Club and Friends of the Earth. She believes that global warming is the single greatest challenge facing humanity today.

Photo Credits

Cover (left) © Nita Winter/The Image Works; cover (right) © www.istockphoto.com/ Stephanie DeLay; cover (bottom), pp. 12, 20 © www.istockphoto.com/Richard Schmidt-Zuper; pp. 5, 25 © AP Photos; p. 6 © www.istockphoto.com/Jaap Hart; p. 7 © Bildarchiv Preussischer Kultbesitz/Art Resource, N.Y.; p. 9 © Newscom; p. 13 © Rachel Epstein/Photo Edit; p. 14 © www.istockphoto.com; p. 15 © www.istockphoto. com/Curt Pickens; p. 18 © Bonnie Kamin/Photo Edit; p. 19 © David R. Frazier/ The Image Works; pp. 21, 23 © www.istockphoto.com/Tomas Bercic; p. 22 © www. istockphoto.com/Ewen Cameron; pp. 27, 28 © www.istockphoto.com/Cheryl Graham; pp. 31, 33 © Shutterstock; pp. 32, 36 © www.istockphoto.com/Pattie Calfy; p. 35 ©AFP/Getty Images; p. 38 © Melissa Carroll.

Designer: Les Kanturek; Photo Researcher: Marty Levick

3 2186 00174 6691

Fossil Ridge Public Library District
Braidwood, IL 60408